Copy Right© 2012 GGP

All Rights Reserved

ISBN-13: **978-1494313791**

Credits:
Illustrator: Ebone Hassan
Page 10 illustrated by Camille S. Nesbit
Illustrating Editor: Ein Fussell
Interviewee: Latanya Denise Wilson

This project could have not been a success without each of you. Thank You so much.

Thanks a bunch
God Is watching

Acknowledgement

First giving all glory to God with a cheerful heart and thankfulness! My spirit could not rest until this book was written and published. To my Husband thanks for dreaming with me and step-by-step living in the dream, the love is unconditional. Thanks to my Mother for giving me her true self no masking or sugar coating. To my three awesome and energetic children Camille, Caylin and Caius you will forever be my joy. Thanks for believing in me when I doubted myself, for pushing me and not letting me have a dull moment.

Special thanks to Terry Y. Davis of Goldin Glow Publishing (terryydavis@yahoo.com) for the opportunity to fulfill my dreams of becoming an "Author" and last but not least thanks to all of my family and close friends that took time to listen and believe in me.

From Me To You

Someone somewhere is having this same experience you are having right now

You are never alone!

Meet Jacob:

Jacob he is a very fun loving kid

who loves wrestling, watching movies, reading and playing

with friends and family.

Jacob is about to experience a new and different event in his life.

He has no idea but it's the lost of his Uncle Michael whom he enjoyed

playing and wrestling with almost as much as he did with his dad.

With this event Jacob experiences the emotions of sadness, anger,

disappointment and loneliness different than any he has in the past.

Jacob will learn about death, and the feelings he's having.

He will also learn ways to cope and bring closure to such an event.

I woke up this morning to a sound of sadness.

"What happened?" I asked. I was told that we would have to travel out of town to meet with the family.

When we arrived everyone was looking sad.

I noticed one person was missing from the crowd, Uncle Michael. Then I heard the news, Uncle Michael died and will not be with me physically on earth to play, talk, race or wrestle anymore.

Then, I began to look and feel sad like everyone else in the room.

The day came for the final gathering. Everyone was dressed up and the atmosphere was quiet.

We rode together in a long car; well most of us rode in the long car. We arrived at the building and there lay Uncle Michael, I was looking at him for the last time.

Seeing Uncle Michael laying there, I began to feel sad, angry and disappointed. Later that day, I sat alone thinking about how I would miss Uncle Michael and that I would never see him again.

Soon Aunt Stacey came over to sit with me. Aunt Stacey and I began to talk about how I was feeling and about never seeing Uncle Michael again.

Aunt Stacey explained to me that dying is a natural part of life for people, animals and all living things. She said that it's something we cannot avoid.

She also said that it was okay to feel sad, angry and disappointed especially when it is a sudden and very new experience.

She told me that I can always talk to my Parents, her, or anyone I feel I can open up to. It would be okay if I asked to speak with a Counselor whenever I need to. She also said to always pray.

She explained prayer is a way we communicate with God.

Aunt Stacey made me feel better about having the feelings I was having and by explaining to me that death is a natural part of life. As the day went on I was able to play with my cousins because I now understood. I understood that it was totally normal to feel angry, sad, disappointed and lonely during a time of losing someone or something you love.

Having this experience and talking to Aunt Stacey helped me to cope with the loss of my loved one.

Although I miss him he remains in my heart. My family and I still talk about the person Uncle Michael was and how much he meant to us.

When my friends say they have had this experience I say "ME TOO" and I share my feeling and how I coped with the loss and grief.

Matthew 5:4
"Blessed are they that mourn: for they shall be comforted."